Water Colours

Water Colours

Photographs by Rosamond Orford

Published by Upcountry Publishing
1485 Union Village Road
Norwich, Vermont 05055
www.upcountrypublishing.com

Printed by The Stinehour Press, Lunenburg, Vermont 05906

Designed by Mim Adkins, www.mimspeak.com

Requests for permission to make copies of any part of the work should be mailed to:
        Upcountry Publishing
        1485 Union Village Road
        Norwich, Vermont 05055

        www.upcountrypublishing.com

WATER COLOURS: photographs by Rosamond Orford
        First edition

ISBN: 0-615-12095-4

for Ford

How much of beauty—of color as well as form—on which our eyes daily rest goes unperceived by us.

—Henry David Thoreau

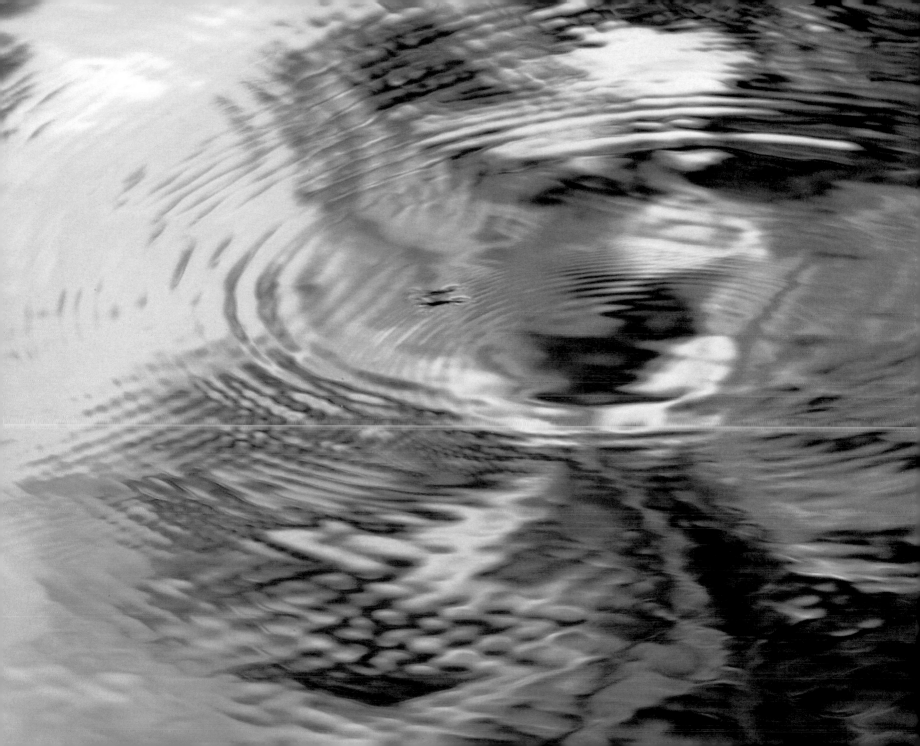

Author's Note

I lived for some years on the banks of the Connecticut River in Vermont and came to love the river's many changes of mood and color — the power and turbulence of the spring run-off, the languid calm of a hot summer day, the rising mists of fall and the fractured icy surfaces of winter. More subtle are its reflections, patterns and rhythms.

Water Colours attempts to capture, on film, images of what is impermanent: the effects of light on water. As I have traveled from my native England to places of great beauty throughout the world, I have also grown to understand the calming and restorative powers of water.

None of the images in this book have been digitally manipulated. All are as I saw them.

My *special thanks* to Florence Fogelin, who gave the book its name and provided invaluable editorial assistance. My gratitude also to Robert C. Dean, Jr., for his unflagging encouragement; and to Judith Bowen for technical help.

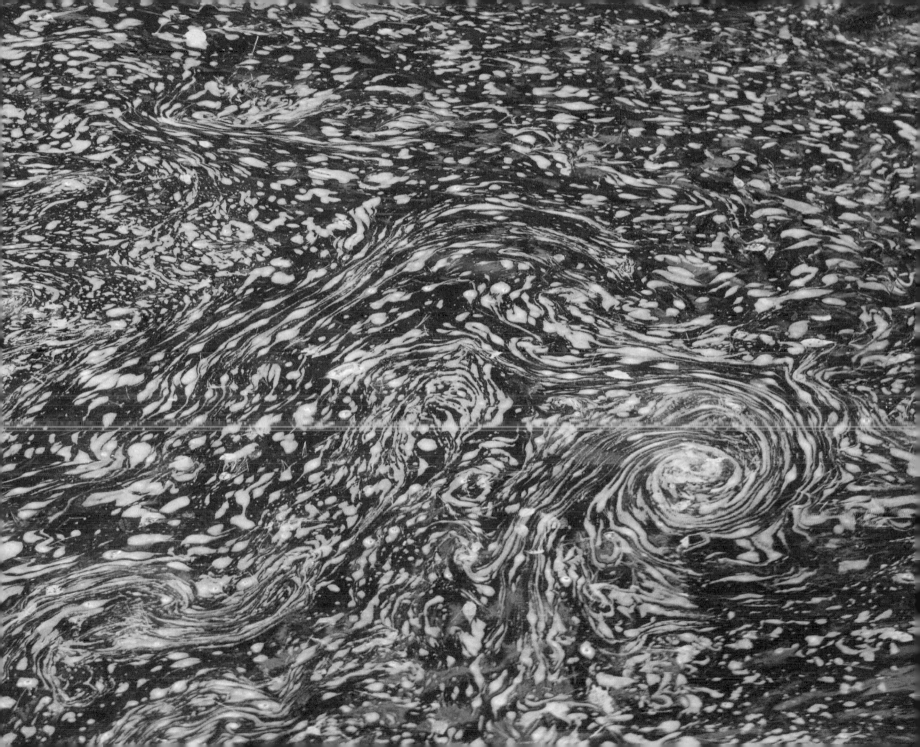

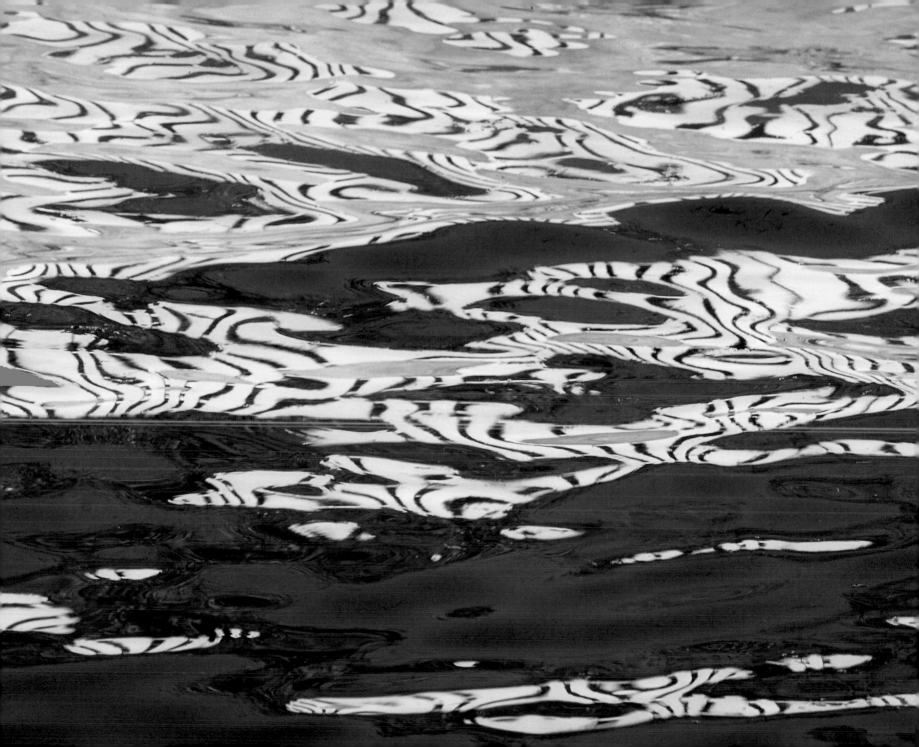

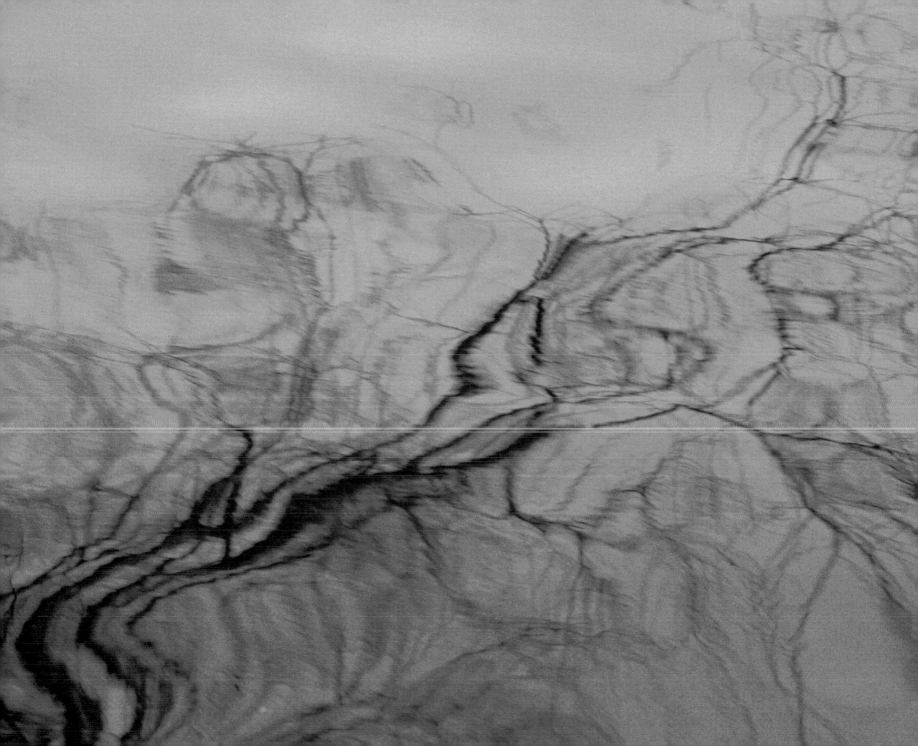

Water Colours Locations

Rosamond Orford, born and educated in England, grew up west of London and spent summers in Cumbria.

After finishing school and accompanying her parents on a trip to Africa, wanderlust led her to explore the wider world. She ended up in the American West in 1963. An avid horsewoman, she worked on dude ranches, picked up odd jobs, traveled, helped run a ski lodge, and began a consuming interest in photography. Following a 1968 move to Vermont, Orford's photography grew into a successful business: Upcountry Cards are sold throughout New England, offering a wide range of views and close-ups of the region's scenery with a distinctive emphasis on its soft light, contours and colors. Largely self-taught, Orford has taken courses with Ernst Haas and Sam Abell. She exhibits widely in New England and has won awards at New Hampshire Art Association shows, most recently in 2001.

Camera in hand, Orford has traveled to Nepal (twice), Crete, Italy, Ecuador, Costa Rica, Galapagos, Mexico, Patagonia and India. She regularly visits the Rocky Mountains and maintains her family home in the English Lake District. Active in the cause of environmental preservation, she led in saving a Vermont river from hydrodevelopment, gaining a settlement to protect and to designate it as a scenic river.

In Water Colours, her first book of photography, Orford draws upon a catalogue of photographs from her travels but largely from more recent work emphasizing abstract patterns, reflections, colors and the play of light on water.

Orford lives in Norwich, Vermont, with her companion, a high school science teacher; with a young student from Nepal she has co-sponsored; and with two "potcake" dogs she brought back from trips to the Bahamas.